Pulse And Paradox

A Chronicle of the Heart's Quietest
Whispers and Loudest Echos

Meghna Mulinti

BookLeaf
Publishing

India | USA | UK

Made with ❤ on the BookLeaf Publishing Platform
www.bookleafpub.in
www.bookleafpub.com

Dedication

This book is dedicated to my husband

My Beautiful Man,

Your heart has an infinite magnitude to give love and inspire millions. Every page in this book carries a piece of what I've grasped from this life with you. You stood by me with unshakable resolve and love when the world seemed to avenge my moral compass. If love from my blood bonds is the closest thing to divine grace, then your presence in my life is the universe's way of answering that prayer twice over.

I need you...

When words cause burns,
When pretty becomes awful,
When cries become common,
When my crew turns sly,
When winters aren't cozy,
When the dawn is ending,

When 'Olaf' is angry,
When bitter is the taste,
When my eyes don't open,
When the sky roars thunders,
When volcanoes erupt,
When hope grows dim.

I need you!

Preface

Life doesn't come with a manual. It comes with wounds that bloom into wisdom and questions that outlive their answers. This book is my love letter to the messy, magnificent act of being alive. Just, breathe as the pages do! Every word written hums that the universe is awaiting you to join her chorus.

Every chapter in this book holds prudence about the depths of calmness. It shows how there are storms you'll learn to sleep through. Not because they vanish, but because you become the calm within them. These poems are my heart's diary. They are the echoes of battles fought in silence. May they arm you for yours.

Acknowledgements

My first debt is to Lord Shri Krishna, the supreme godhead, whose solicitude led me to explore life paths I never could have, without his omnipotence. His benevolence unwrapped noval horizons and equipped me with great revelations of life. At his feet, I lay my foremost gratitude.

I'm eternally grateful to my husband, the keeper of my flame—who has been steadfast in everything I do in life. Unique to this book, he has been the untiring advocate of my ability to express and emote gracefully. His zeal in stepping up for my aspirations constantly nudges me to taste an unparalleled life experience.

I owe an everlasting gratitude to my mother, my first oracle, who has always been a solid adherent of my idiosyncratic endeavors. Her lessons, fierce and tender, carved in raw honesty, are the bedrock upon which I stand. And my father, my staunch supporter, whose quiet pride is the castle around my dreams.

I'm indebted to my little sister, a pocket-sized sage, who has stretched my world beyond measure with her galaxies of wisdom. She showed me acuity wears no size, and love no bounds.

My gratitude is infinite to my grandparents. Their hands held mine when I was small; now their insight holds my heart. To be loved by them is to know the purest kind of belonging. Their stories and sacrifices shaped me into the woman that I am. Some bonds transcend time—their's is etched into my bones.

Just as importantly, I'm forever in the universe's debt, for fitting me in her grand scheme of chance and destiny. I kneel in awe at this improbable, exquisite journey.

1. Built, Not Born

Confidence is a flame inside,
A steady glow, a quiet guide.
It asks for time, it seeks your trust,
It grows in love, it fights off rust.

It's not in luck, it's not in fate,
Confidence is what you create.
Not just a trait, not just a name,
But practice wrapped in steady flame.

Each moment bold, each choice you make,
Is proof of all the steps you take.
Not in your genes, but in your fight,
A skill that shines, a burning light.

It's not a thread woven in birth,
But proof of how you shape your worth.
Each time you show up, speak and do,
You tell the world, "I value me too."

It's how you walk, how you stand,
The way you take life in your hand.
It's telling YOU, "I've got your back",
And stepping forward, never slack.

They say it's in your blood, your name,
But confidence is not a claim.
It's taught, it's learned, it's made with care,
It's something strong yet light as air.

It's not a gift from fate or chance,
But a rhythm you learn, a steady dance.
With every step, with every try,
It lifts your voice, it lets you fly.

2. The Universe Listens

The universe listens, the universe sees,
She feels your wishes in every breeze.
When you give with love, with truth, with grace,
She sends it back in time and space.

The friend who called when days felt low,
The chance that came when you let go.
The kindness sown, the good you spread,
Returns in ways you never read.

A job you missed, a door once closed,
Perhaps a path yet undisclosed.
A love that left, a tear you wept,
She saw it all, the faith you kept.

The dream you chased, the risk you took,
The lessons written in your book.
They all align, they find their way,
She moves them closer day by day.

When dreams feel distant, lost in the sky,
The universe whispers, "Just give it a try."
She moves the stars, she shifts the tide,
Align your heart—she walks beside.

She hears your hopes, she feels your fears,
She gathers whispers through the years.
The loss you mourn, the days so tough,
She molds them into gold and love.

Trust the flow, align your way,
The universe gives—you just have to say.
So lift your heart, embrace the view,
The universe is shaping you.

3. The Gift Within the Storm

Once, you cursed the nights so long,
Where echoes of your past felt wrong.
You ran from grief, you fought its chains,
Yet found yourself in loops of pain.

The storm arrived, unkind, unplanned,
It stole the ground beneath your stand.
You fought, you screamed, you cursed the sky,
But pain just watched, with knowing eyes.

Pain is fire, fierce and wild,
It burns the lost, the hurt, the child.
But in its heat, a change is on,
A brighter soul, a heart reborn.

Pain is a sculptor, rough yet wise,
It chisels truth and removes disguise.
You lose, you break, you fall apart,
Yet find the masterpiece—your heart.

The job denied, the friend who strayed,
The moments where you felt betrayed.
Each taught a lesson, deep and raw,
Each unveiled wisdom, turned to awe.

The love that left, the dream that fell,
The silent wars you knew too well.
Each scar it carved, each tear it stole,
Yet through the cracks, it shaped your soul.

Then pain spoke soft, "Stay for a while,
Look within, release denial."
So you did, and there you found,
The path was built on hollow ground.

Pain did not come just to destroy,
It carved out a room for depth and joy.
For pain does not just crush and tear,
It builds, it shapes, it makes you rare.

4. The Calm Answer

When tempers flare and voices rise,
Pause and listen to the quiet phase.
Don't let the moment make you shout in vain,
Respond with thought, let wisdom reign.

Listen, when chaos comes to play,
And the day turns sour in a blink of gray.
Don't react on impulse, don't let fear dictate;
Instead, respond with calm—recalibrate.

Think of the moment when words cut like a knife,
A criticism that stings more than strife.
Rather than lashing out in a storm of pain,
You choose to reply, "I've learned from this gain."

You often face a world that tests your will,
Where every wrong might seem to echo still.
When anger flares and reactions seem so near,
Remember: respond, and let your thoughts steer.

Like when your coffee spills on a busy day,
Or plans become suddenly stray,
You tell yourself, "I care for myself enough to choose
A path of calm, where no rebuttal can bruise."

Imagine the rush when your path falls apart,
A canceled outing or a friend who's late to start.
Instead of a snap full of dread,
You whisper, "This too shall pass," and tread.

Standing at life's twisting door,
Feel anger knock, but you choose to explore.
Not every bump in the road is a curse;
Respond with grace, let each moment reverse.

Take a breath and give your mind its time,
To sift through turmoil and find a rhyme.
When things go wrong, say, "All's well, my heart can handle,
This storm is a teacher, not just a scandal."

In that pause, you find the truth inside:
Every trial is a chance to grow and rise.
Your heart, resilient, tells you every wound
Can blossom into wisdom, once understood.

5. Whispers of the Turning Tide

Change is the thread that weaves through your days,
A silent metamorphosis in countless ways.
Imagine a moment when success crowns your name,
Then a sudden twist erases that fleeting fame.

When the winds of transformation begin to blow,
They scatter the certainties you thought you'd know.
Today, you might ride high on a crest of delight,
Tomorrow, find the path obscured in the night.

Like blossoms that bloom then gracefully fall,
Each shift, each season, enriches us all.
Embrace the lesson: change builds strength inside,
A resilient spirit that's ready for every ride.

Mother Nature shows us with every sunrise,
That change is constant, a truth so wise.
Today you might revel in riches or renown,
But like the tide receding from the shore of town,

What once was grand may softly fade away,
A lesson learned in each shifting day.

Just as trees shed leaves to grow anew,
Accept each change, and let resilience guide you.
In every ending, a fresh beginning is spun,
A cycle of life where every loss is won.

Like a caterpillar that dares to dream of flight,
Or a river redirecting under moonlit night,
Every shift, however stark it may seem,
Builds resilience, fuels the spirit's realm.

Life's journey is painted with strokes to switch,
Moments of glory, and setbacks that feel too rich.
Today, you're at the peak, embraced by light,
Tomorrow, shadows may gently steal the sight.

Think of summer's warmth yielding to winter's chill,
Each season's passage teaches us strength and will.
So embrace the rhythm, the ebb and the flow,
Change writes the verses of all you know.

6. The Mirror of Your Mind

You hold a secret power deep inside,
A spark that turns dreams into your guide.
When you believe, your heart aligns,
Creating a world that truly shines.

Imagine a painter with a canvas bare,
Every stroke is born of hope and care.
Believe in the colors, let passion lead,
And watch as life transforms from seed to deed.

Witness the leader who stood tall and brave,
Who believed in change and the lives they'd save.
Through storms and trials, they held their ground
In the kingdom of belief, true strength is found.

When doubt arises, and shadows confine,
Remember: belief is the power that refines.
With every brave step, with every new scene,
You grow stronger—with a thought so keen.

Your belief is an empire, vast and grand,
Where every thought is sculpted by your hand.
When you choose the good and embrace your dream,
The impossible becomes part of your theme.

Look in the mirror—what do you see?
A reflection of the faith that sets you free.
If you trust in your power to grow,
Your soul aligns, and greatness will show.

You set out each day with a vision in mind,
Belief as your compass, uniquely designed.
Listen close, let your spirit sing,
For your heart sees the verity of everything.

Let each thought be a brick in your design,
A fortress of hope where your principles align.
So nurture your dreams with steadfast might,
Transforming darkness into radiant light.

Remember, you become what you believe in,
A palace of wonder that you're destined to win.

7. A Touch of the Present

Mountains rise, valleys sink,
You chase the highs—yet, stop and think
What if joy is not in heights,
But in steady, golden lights?

The crunch of leaves, a morning run,
The sparkle in the setting sun.
You miss it all when you delay,
Waiting for another day.

Don't lose yourself in what once was,
Or chase the future just because.
The past is gone, the future unknown,
But this moment? It's yours alone.

A child laughs, the sun feels warm,
The breeze hums a gentle form.
If you pause, if you stay,
You'll find life singing today.

You celebrate wins, you mourn what's lost,
Tell me, is it worth the cost?
While you cling to yesterdays,
Life unfolds in quiet ways.

A bird in flight, a sip of tea,
The way the rain hums endlessly.
Not in the past, not in dreams,
Life exists in simple streams.

Why race ahead? Why rewind?
Why get lost inside your mind?
Life is neither then nor when,
It only happens now, my friend.

Give your all to what's in sight,
Not to what has taken flight.
Your trophies gleam, your past may ache,
But life's a wave, not a lake.

Forget the hills, forget the fall,
The plateau binds it all.
Right here, right now—this is where,
You truly breathe, you truly fare.

Let the present be your art,
It's the only place to start.

Stay a while, let go of 'when'
This moment won't return again.

15

8. Walk a Mile in Their Shoes

The shoes of another may pinch and may bind,
But walking in them opens the mind.
To feel their blisters, to know their pace,
To see the world shaped by their unique case.

Every soul has a path to tread,
A mountain to climb, a fear to shed.
When we pause to listen, to truly hear,
We build a connection, crystal clear.

For every tear, there's a story to tell,
A battle fought, a tolling bell.
When we step into their world, we see,
The beauty of shared humanity.

Compassion grows with every stride,
A bridge of hope, a gentle tide.
So take their hand, and you'll soon find,
The strength to heal, the heart to be kind.

For every stumble, there's a tale to share,
A heft to carry, a cross to bear.
Their steps may falter, their balance may break,
But in their shoes, we feel their ache.

In the mirror of empathy, we truly see,
The reflections of others, their pain, their glee.
A crack in their smile, a tear in their eye,
A spiel of struggle and their silent try.

Take a step into their room to feel the quiet,
Carry their burden, share their fate.
Knowledge blooms when we dare to care,
When we open our hearts and choose to be there.

Empathy is a muscle, it grows each day,
With every step, we learn to stay.
Slip on their shoes, take a walk, take a stand,
And hold out your heart with an open hand.

The world grows softer, the edges less sharp,
When we light the way with a benevolent spark.
So look in the mirror, and you'll soon find,
The weight of walking in someone else's mind.

9. The Circle of Control

Power is not a chaplet of gold to wear,
But a flame that flickers, a cross to bear.
With every king who rules the land,
A greater force shapes the shifting sand.

The spider spins, the lion roars,
Yet storms can shake their mighty doors.
With power comes a fragile thread,
To wield it wisely, or fall instead.

The teacher shapes the minds of youth,
The doctor heals with hands of truth.
Still, they must humbly bow,
To forces greater, here and now.

Power is a flame, both fierce and bright,
A tool to build or burn the night.
The leader stands, the world in view,
But knows the winds can shift anew.

Power is a scale, a balance fine,
A gift, a curse, a fragile line.
The judge who wields the gavel's might,
Must weigh the wrongs against the right.

Power is a circle, never complete,
A dance of strength and humble feet.
The one who builds the bridge,
Must answer to the river's ridge.

The parent guides the child's way,
Yet knows the world will have its say.
The poet writes with words so grand,
But silence holds the upper hand.

Seek to know, let wisdom grow,
Power blooms when you're ready to flow.
With every act, the choice is yours,
To open or to lock the doors.

Hold the flame with steady care,
Power is the weight of your chair.
Let knowledge guide, let wisdom lead,
To plant the seeds of a noble deed.

Look for light, let insight grow,
Power thrives where wisdom flows.

With every step, the burden stays,
So, use it well throughout your days.

10. Wolves in Gilded Robes

Charity balls and grand displays,
Yet hunger roams in unseen ways.
The photos shine, the ribbons glow,
But still, the children starve below.

They sign the checks, they cut the tape,
Not knowing if their acts really shape.
A heart that beats for public view
Was never warm, it never knew.

Work hard, they say, and you shall rise,
Yet gatekeepers hold all the ties.
They mock the poor for lacking more,
Then slam shut every open door.

They teach you peace, they preach you love,
Then drop the bombs from up above.
They say the forests need more care,
Then sign the deals that strip them bare.

They shame the poor for seeking bread,
While drowning in the gold they shed.
Their lips spill honey, sweet and kind,
Yet leave a bitter taste behind.

They say the law is blind and fair,
But wealth decides who gets a chair.
A thief who steals to feed his kin
Finds iron bars and years within.

But men in suits with silver lies
Can drain the poor and still rise high.
They call it fraud, but not for them
A business move will do the whim.

You see their lies, you hear their schemes,
But tell me—are you what you seem?
You curse the leaders, scorn the throne,
Yet leave your fellow man alone.

You beg for change but fear the cost,
For comfort's gain, the fight is lost.
Before you cast the first of stones,
Look deep within—what have you shown?

You learn the game is far from fair,
But in the cracks, you still must dare.

You see that merit isn't real,
Yet still, you fight, yet still, you feel.

23

The kindness done for eyes alone
Is but a shadow, cold as stone.
Hypocrisy thrives in every face,
Change starts with you, not some far place.

11. Be the Puddle, Be the Sea

Poured into a glass, you sit so still,
Yet in a river, you rush with will.
You feed the trees, you drown the land,
You soften stone, you create strand.

You slip into a cup, a bowl, a stream,
No questions asked, no shattered dream.
A waterfall, you carve the rock,
You sit in silence, when there's no knock.

A drizzle falls, the earth revives,
A flood arrives, and nothing thrives.
The sea can gift, the sea can take,
Still never questions its own fate.

A pot, a pond, a mighty wave,
Each form you take is one you gave.
You never fight the shape you're in,
You know you're meant to win.

They built a dam to hold you tight,
You gathered strength and rose in height.
They caged you in, they drew the lines,
But, river, you don't obey designs.

You wait, you slip, you shape, you grow,
You crack the land, yet let it flow.
No need for war, no need for rage,
You move mountains proud with age.

You sit in a lake, the sky stares back,
You rage in a storm, the ships lose track.
You whisper in mist, you roar in rain,
Never once do you complain.

You do not ask, 'Why am I here?'
You simply shift from clear to sheer.
In each form, in each disguise,
You still remain—no compromise.

Conquer yourself, let go of pride,
And watch the world fall to your stride.
Adapt with ease, don't fight the mold,
Your strength is quiet, yet uncontrolled.

Shape your soul, shift with grace,

And elegance will offer you its place.
Do not resist, stay still to break,
The world is yours for you to take.

12. Brave Enough to Care

They say the world rewards the fierce,
That strength is built in iron and spears.
But tell me, have you ever tried
To stand with love when hate's applied?

To meet a wound with tender care,
To give when no one else would dare?
It takes no strength to strike and break,
But kindness—that's the war you stake.

The loudest voices rarely know
That power lies in what you show.
To walk away, to mend, to heal,
To offer warmth the world won't steal.

It's easy to reflect the pain,
To meet the dark with more disdain.
But those who stand despite the storm
Are those whose hearts refuse to conform.

To love yourself is not a crime,
Nor selfish act, nor waste of time.
Only when your roots are deep
Can you give shade for souls to keep.

No need to match, no need to weigh,
You run your race in your own way.
Not better, worse, or lost in pride,
Just growing more with each new stride.

You do not fight, you do not plead,
You only give where love is freed.
No score to keep, no race to run,
Just kindness shared with everyone.

Kindness blooms in those who dare
To face the world yet still repair.
It bends, it breaks, yet grows again,
Not out of fear, but love within.

The strongest ones do not compare,
They rise by lifting others there.
Stay soft, stay kind, yet never yield,
Strength is found where hearts are healed.

To stand unshaken in your grace,
Is proof that love is not a chase.

The ones who grow, the ones who thrive,
Are those who let their love survive.

29

13. Where the Tide Slows Down

The world is loud, it pulls, it sways,
It steals your time in endless ways.
But step away, just for a while,
And meet yourself beyond the dial.

The quiet holds a room so wide,
Where thoughts no longer need to hide.
Here, you mend, you breathe, you grow,
A world within that few will know.

A painter stares at the canvas bare,
A poet stops mid-thought, mid-air.
A thinker drifts through tangled streams,
Each lost within their silent dreams.

Alone, you meet yourself at last,
Beyond the rush, beyond the past.
Nothing to cloud your mind,
Just truth in silence, raw, refined.

A storm rolls loud, the voices swell,
The noise outside, you know it well.
But somewhere past the crashing tide,
A silent shore awaits inside.

You sit, you breathe, you face your fears,
The ones long drowned in busy years.
Yet in this space, no need to flee,
Solitude lets you be free.

The world may pull, demand, insist,
That every moment must exist
In crowded halls, in words and calls,
No space to hear yourself at all.

But solitude's a garden wide,
Where thoughts can bloom, unchained, untied.
A place to rest, to clear, to see,
To be alone, still feel free.

Solitude is the artist's muse,
A land where thoughts have room to choose.
No noise to steal, no rush, no race,
Just time to dance on a vacant base.

In solitude, the waters clear,

The thoughts you lost come back sincere.
The heart slows down, the mind can mend,
And in that pause, you find a friend.

When life grows loud, don't chase the roar,
Find peace within, upon your shore.
In stillness, let your mind explore,
A brave new world opening its core.

When all is still and time is new,
The only voice you hear is you.
Step back, step in, embrace the air,
You'll find yourself still waiting there.

14. The Treasure is in the Climb

A farmer sows his golden seeds,
With steady hands and patient deeds.
He does not count how fast they grow,
But tends the earth, steady and slow.

The rains may come, the sun may hide,
Yet still, he works, with trust as a guide.
Then one bright day, his fields stand tall,
With grains of gold—the reward for all.

A runner does not stop mid-race,
To check how far he's set the pace.
He looks ahead, firm and true,
His only thought: push through, push through.

Not once he wonders 'Have I won?'
Before the finish line is done.
He simply runs, swift and free,
And finds the medal chasing thee.

A painter strokes the canvas bare,
With focus deep and thoughtful care.
He does not pause at every line,
To seek if beauty starts to shine.

He moves, he blends, his heart beats fast,
In love with work, he holds it vast.
And when at last the work is done,
He turns to see—a prize well won.

So paint your life with steady hands,
Don't seek the praise, don't shift your stance.
Those who work with heart and soul,
Will find success in full control.

So play your tune, don't seek the prize,
The world will hear when the skill will rise.
Those who love the work they do,
Will find success come chasing too.

Work each day, give all your best,
Let go of fear, forget the rest.
When your roots in effort lie,
The fruits of labor come by and by.

Take your steps, one by one,

And let the race itself be fun.
When you chase what's done with grace,
Success will meet you—face to face.

15. The Quiet Observer

Speak less, they say, and watch them all,
The rise in pride, the fearsome fall.
A careless tongue may fan the flame,
But silence shields you from the blame.

A word unspoken lingers still,
A choice unmade, a quiet will.
The echoes of what might have been,
A secret song beneath the din.

You tell them all, they nod, they smile,
But judgment hides beneath the while.
A tale too soon, a careless share,
And now your thoughts are theirs to bear.

A crowded room, a thousand eyes,
Some crave the stage, some seek to disguise.
But those who pause, who watch, who see,
They grasp the world from a zone judgment-free.

A secret kept is a garden grown,
Roots unbound and seeds unknown.
The world may pry, but let them yearn,
Some facts are best for you to learn.

Share a smile, a fleeting glance,
But not each thought, not every chance.
For words once spilled may twist and turn,
And gift regrets we can't return.

They ask you why you walk alone,
No tales to weave, no seeds you've sown.
But solitude, a tender friend,
Will guard your truths until the end.

No burdened gaze, no judging eyes,
Just steady ground and open skies.
Unchained from what the mob expects,
A heart at peace, a mind reflects.

Observe the whispers, learn the game,
What's real is rarely said the same.
A thousand faces, stories spun,
Yet watchful eyes outshine the sun.

Watch the stage with players bold,
Not all your stories must be told.

In stillness lies a quiet grace,
A power that time cannot erase.

In silence blooms a wiser voice,
A clearer path, a calmer choice.
So keep some chapters yet unread,
Not all words are meant to be spread.

Hold steady ground, unveil no scheme,
Not every thought must chase a dream.
The quiet soul will stand apart,
A fortress built with a guarded heart.

Silence blooms like morning light,
A shield against the prying night.
Not all should know your deepest tune,
Some facts are best beneath the moon.

You hold your words like precious gold,
With some stories young, some much old.
But not each ear can bear their weight,
Objective verity is best to contemplate.

To speak is a choice, to share is bold,
But silence too can break the mold.
A careful voice, a measured tone,
And soon, you'll find a mind of your own.

16. Freedom in the Unsaid

They struck you once, but not again,
You broke the chains and escaped the pain.
No words to throw, no fight to start,
Just silence now — a work of art.

They wanted screams, a vengeful call,
A shattered pride, a final brawl.
But words would only bind you near,
You chose to rise, not linger here.

No need for venom, sharp and cold,
No tales of hurt are left retold.
You smiled through tears and strolled away,
Your silence has the final say.

A thousand words could wage a war,
But none would heal the inner scar.
You leave them sealed, unheard,
A swordless fight needs no word.

You did not shout, you raised no hand,
No vicious scheme, no reprimand.
You simply left — no grand parade,
A quiet charm that won't degrade.

They search for flames to feed the fight,
But you have learned to stray from spite.
Your anger's now a distant song,
Growth has made you twice as strong.

You left the ashes, scorched and gray,
And built a world that blooms today.
No longing glance, no backward tread,
Their name no longer haunts your head.

While they wait to hear your cries,
You chase the sun in endless skies.
And in your void, they understand,
Your silence speaks; you've won unmanned.

They wish for storms to crash and burn,
But you have wiser ways to turn.
Each bitter thought, you let release,
Silence is your only peace.

No louder act than walking free,
No sweeter sound than dignity.

While they expect you fall or cry,
You stand unbowed, you silence high.

They wait for rage to claim its throne,
But you've outgrown what once was known.
Each ounce of hurt, you laid to rest,
In stillness, you became your best.

No bitter cries, no wasted breath,
You found your peace, you mocked their wrath.
And in your calm, they'll one day see,
Your silence was the loss to be.

While they await some bitter sound,
You stand on unshakable ground.
Their echoes call, yet none reply,
Still alive is the quietest goodbye.

17. A Sky Full of You

They'll stand and speak of you in the past tense,
A eulogy of fragments, a life condensed.
But how can they capture the nights you cried,
The battles fought, the dreams denied?

They'll try to chart the map of your years,
But charts can't show the sweat, the tears.
The roads you walked with no one near,
The whispers of doubt you chose not to hear.

They'll pluck a few flowers from your garden of time,
A rose to honor your work, a lily to celebrate your
prime.
But how can they know the roots you grew,
In soil unshared, where no one knew?

They'll play a tune at your final bow,
A melody of what they think they can show.
But how can they capture the notes unsung,
The battles fought, the songs unstrung?

They'll point to stars and call them yours,
A constellation of triumphs and wars.
But how can they trace the light you shed,
Through galaxies of dreams, you once fled?

The path you walked was yours alone,
Through storms of judgment, seeds were sown.
Instruction like thunder, ideas like rain,
Yet you grew forests in the pain.

Alone, you faced the cacophony's roar,
Suggestions that clashed, criticism that tore.
You still built a compass from your own spine,
And followed its needle, a path divine.

Solas, you planted in the quiet of night,
Through noise and chaos, you sought the light.
Advice like weeds smears like frost,
And, you bloomed where others were lost.

You walked unescorted through the noise and din,
A symphony of silence deep within.
You charted a course only you could see,
A universe of growth, wild and free.

At the end, they'll say, "They lived, they died,"

But the history of your soul is too vast to guide.
You've arrived when your story outgrows the page,
A legacy too fierce to cage.

No sun can capture your glow,
The struggles, the triumphs, the ebbs, the flow.
You've arrived when your sky outshines the view,
A constellation too infinite to construe.

No speech can hold the weight of your climb,
The silent victories, the stolen time.
You've arrived when you don't fit a vessel,
With the tale of your heritage as vast as a castle.

18. The Platinum Rule of Your Mind

Your thoughts are threads both dark and light,
They weave your days and shape your night.
A fleeting fear, a hopeful call,
They paint the rise, they break the fall.

Within your mind, a garden grows,
Of towering hopes and shadowed lows.
Each thought you plant will break the ground,
And bloom in joy or fear unbound.

A sculptor hides within your soul,
With steady hands that shape you whole.
Each fear you nurse, each joy you crave,
It molds your path, bold and brave.

The world you see is not just real,
But shaped by thoughts you dare to feel.
A whispered whirlwind, a shadowed doubt,
And all you dread comes reaching out.

Yet in your mind, a spark remains,
A seed of hope through joy and pain.
You choose to dream, you choose to trust,
To break the chains of fear and dust.

When worry knocks and doubts arise,
You close your weary, searching eyes.
You see instead what could be true,
A sky reborn in boundless blue.

A trembling fear, a bitter deed,
Will only sprout in tangled greed.
But faith — it falls like golden rain,
And fills the soil of thought again.

You weed the doubt, you mend the break,
And bloom in truths you dare to make.
In your hands, both far and near,
The laurels of belief appear.

A storm may rise within your chest,
A restless doubt, a gale suppressed.
But thoughts like stars can pierce the night,
And flood the dark with ancient light.

You're no pawn to fate's demand,

Your dreams are charts, your thoughts command.
A shift in mind, a spark of grace,
And horror dissolves without a trace.

Each step you take, the fabric grows,
Of what you seek and what you know.
The path you weave is yours to tread,
A journey born of thoughts you've fed.

With faith you walk, with trust you stand,
Like a sailor on a boundless land.
What you think, you soon shall find,
The world obeys your fearless mind.

19. Tranquility's Trust Fund

They tried to break the sky you see,
But stars still shine relentlessly.
A thousand doubts, a thousand lies,
Yet none could dim your endless tries.

They tried to shape you with disdain,
To bind joy, to stake their claim.
But words are echoes in the wind,
And you decide what voice you send.

A castle stands tall within your soul,
Untouched by words you can't control.
They hurl their doubts, they crave your fear,
But walls of worth stay strong and clear.

They spoke with words both sharp and loud,
To break your strength, to draw a crowd.
But you stood still as a beaming ray,
You faded their flame with a silent slay.

A name they gave, a scornful call,
None of it could make you fall.
You decide what words shall stay,
The rest are wind that blows away.

A million names and a billion sneers,
None could shake your guarded years.
You're not what others quote,
Your truth is firm to keep you afloat.

You let their words drift through the air,
They held no weight, they found no care.
Names can only make their mark,
When you invite them through the dark.

No wound can form from hollow spite,
When you refuse to yield your sight.
The vestige wanes, the noise is through,
Your focus shifts to just a few.

Their words were thorns, their stares were cold,
But you held the gospel unsold.
No whispers harm, no judgments stay,
Unless you choose to walk their way.

They called you less, they said you were wrong,
Yet you stood tall, your spirit strong.

Names are powerless and small,
Unless you choose to heed them all.

When wrath unfolds,
Your fear gets told.
Inside you lives a firm compass,
Gleaming bright through all your flaws.

Your mind and life clone in parallel,
Look within, make the ultimate call.
Hold nothing in others' speech,
The citadel lies within your reach.

20. The Phoenix's Ashes

You slipped, you fell, the world looked on,
But failure's just the prelude to dawn.
Each tumble a step in a dance you're learning,
Each bruise a fire, each scrape a burning.

You stumbled hard, you felt belittled,
But defeat is a new fold to your next bold.
Each misstep a spark, each fall a flame,
A forge where courage absorbs its name.

Each plummet leaves your knees bruised and raw,
The mountain laughed, but you ignored its flaw.
For every slip, wisdom was sown,
A draw of the path you'd call your own.

You fell to ashes, the fire burned bright,
But dearth is just the phoenix's flight.
Each ember a drill, each flame a guide,
A plot to the heights where dreams reside.

The ben is high, the air is thin,
But you've been here, you'll soar again.
Quitting is the only true defeat,
The rest are stories, bittersweet.

You've carved before, you'll carve anew,
Collapse is just the artist's glue.
You've risen before, you'll rise again,
Fill this crash as the ink in your pen.

So clasp the falls, the breaks, the scars,
They're just the shadows of the stars.
The peak is steep, but so is your will,
Each fall a stroke, each rise a thrill.

Gather the ashes, the sparks, the pain,
They're just the fuel for your next campaign.
The pinnacle is high, but it's still in view,
Each trough a step, each crest a breakthrough.

So dance with the valleys, embrace the sting,
They're just the twins of your wings.
Each slump a note, destined for just a few,
The summit is tall, but so are you!

21. Miles of Meaning

A stream runs swift and slow,
Not bound by where it aims to go.
It bends and turns without regret,
A silver path, forever set.

It greets the stones that block its way,
Then hums along without delay.
The banks may shift, the course may change,
Yet still it flows, both free and strange.

The mountain calls, the trail unwinds,
A thousand steps, a million finds.
Eyes on the peak, the sky so blue,
But joy blooms bright in what you do.

The breeze that whirs a secret song,
The sturdy trees that stand so strong.
Each rock you climb, each stone you tread,
Your mental muscle grows to keep you ahead.

Don't fix your gaze on heights alone,
The whispering woods remain unknown.
But feel the earth beneath your stride,
The journey's pulse will take the lead.

The clouds may break, the rain may fall,
But it's all green despite it all.
The joy is not the bud's debut,
It's in the drops that kiss the dew.

For those who wait for petals bright,
May miss the sun's most golden light.
Love the seeds you've sown,
Find beauty in what has simply grown.

Runners lost in a fleeting prize,
Forget the joy in the morning skies.
But those who greet the breeze with glee,
Will find they run eternally.

Eyes that long for the ocean's view,
Miss all the ether reflected blue.
To flow is joy, to drift is wise,
Odysseys live in open highs.

22. The Babbling Brook

A hollow drum beats loud and clear,
Makes an empty sound the world will hear.
It boasts of tunes it cannot play,
Still drowns out words with much to say.

A shallow brook is a chatter-bee,
It dances loud for all to see.
But rivers deep move strong and wide,
Their power flows in quiet stride.

The empty cup may rattle well,
Its hollow clang is a boastful bell.
But those who hold the richest wine,
Need not declare their grand design.

A forest stands, strong and still,
The ancient oak upon the hill.
It does not shout to prove its might,
Roots speak louder than the height.

A crow declared, "Behold my flight!
The sky obeys my wings of might!"
It cawed and screeched from tree to tree,
Proclaiming truths none dared to see.

Come the night, an owl took wing,
No praise nor pride upon a string.
With knowing eyes, it scanned the ground,
A hunter's skill is sharp and sound.

A spark ignites with boastful light,
It leaps and flares to claim the night.
It crackles loud, consumes with pride,
But leaves mere ash where once it tried.

Yet embers glow with muted grace,
Their warmth endures through time and space.
They do not blaze to steal the gaze,
But offer light in quiet ways.

Near the shore, the pebbles roared,
Each wave their fleeting strength restored.
They tumbled loudly, they crashed in vain,
Yet left no mark for all their strain.

A stone sat firm beside the sea,
Did not boast of what it could be.

No storm could shake its weathered face,
A monument of a powerful brace.

Hollow words, like the restless tide,
Can never match what truths are tied.
And silent strength will always stay,
Long after the noise has washed away.

Heed the flame that burns too bright,
It seeks no truth but claims the right.
While sagacity hums in a steady tone,
A strength unpraised, but deeply known.

Wisdom wears a humble hue,
And speaks in tones both soft and true.
While echoes fade, the remains,
They roar a voice worth more than empty claims.

23. She Loves Without Words

The soil that births the gleaming grain,
The clouds burst to bring the rain.
A cradle vast, both wild and free,
She holds us all — the land, the sea.

A sparrow's flight, a cloud's embrace,
A woodland deer in a muted chase.
A tide that bows upon the sand,
The throb that moves through sea and land.

The blues unweave a crimson thread,
The sun departs and the day is shed.
Still, the stars will rise and shine,
A constant gift, a grand design.

The sun unfurls in a golden hue,
A gift each day, both old and new.
The breeze that bends the wheat with care,
A muttered song beyond the stare.

The jungle hums with life unseen,
A thousand shades of endless green.
The mountains stand with ancient pride,
Their secrets were kept, their time untied.

A river carved a path in stone,
With patience vast, with strength unknown.
It quenched the thirst of field and tree,
A stream of life eternally.

The bees thrum low, the petals rise,
A bloom unfolds beneath the cries.
The drizzle drops soft, the mists retreat,
Scores of gifts beneath our feet.

The tree stands tall, with arms outspread,
Countless leaves above your head.
It weaves the air for you to breathe,
A perk unseen, yet all receive.

The deep stirs in rhythmic grace,
A boundless blue, a vast embrace.
It feeds the shore, it cools the land,
A precious touch, a giving hand.

Eyes that seek with a selfish view,

Forget the old, forget the true.
Oh, learn from leaves, from streams that run,
And know what wonders Earth has spun.

Hands that tear and eyes that close,
Forget the roots from which life grows.
Earth gives all, both great and small,
And asks but love — the least of all.

Humankind with hurried stride,
Forgets the gifts that time can't hide.
Oh, pause to hear the robin's tune,
And thank the earth, the sky, the moon.

24. For the One Who Feels Like Home

I knew you long before we met,
Like a distant song, I can't forget.
The stars conspired, the winds aligned,
To lead me to the soul I'd find.

We laughed through rain, we danced through doubt,
A love the storms could not put out.
You knew my fears, my wildest schemes,
And cheered the weight of all my dreams.

You read the lines upon my face,
Each joy, each scar I can't erase.
Things to you, I'll confide,
True, our love lives and won't subside.

No pretense here, no need to prove,
You are my stillness when I move.
Through every fault, through every scar,
You loved me just the way you are.

And even when we stand apart,
I feel your presence in my heart.
Soulmates know, without a sound,
Wherever lost, we will be found.

We wander roads, rough and wide,
Yet never lose the other's side.
Through tangled words and bruising nights,
We find a way through life's bites.

In your gaze, I stand complete,
With a brimming rhythm, a steady beat.
A spark that burns but doesn't fade,
A soul whose warmth is never to trade.

You know the deluge I've tried to hide,
Yet love the waves I hold inside.
With every flaw you trace and see,
You choose the depths that make me, me.

And when the world forgets our song,
We'll find the tune we knew all along.
Soulmates stay through joy and pain,
A thousand times, and once again.